DAILY LESSONS FROM

Save-My-Life School

NATALIE HARRIS

PUBLISHED BY WINTERTICKLE PRESS

echo
BOOKS

DAILY LESSONS FROM
Save-My-Life School

"Save-My-Life School" credit: Amanda Barrowcliffe

Cover photo credit: Heather Down

Cover and book design credit: Heather Down

Acquisition credit: Kim Forster

Font credit for Save-My-Life School: Hesster Moffett font, lisensed from joebobgraphics.com

Library and Archives Canada Cataloguing in Publication Data is available upon request.

ISBN 978-1-894813-93-8

Printed in Canada

Published by
Wintertickle Press
Barrie, Ontario, Canada
winterticklepress.com

AUTHOR ACKNOWLEDGEMENT

I would like to credit and thank
the Buddhist Centre, the medical
professionals, the peer groups, the mental
health programs, my friends and my family
who have contributed to the ideas in this
book, both directly and indirectly.

This is a book of quotations based on
and inspired by the writings of Natalie
Harris in her book *Save-My-Life School*.
It is designed so the reader will read
only one concept or lesson per day.
Each page is a single concept, which
is perfect for personal meditation,
reflection, inspiration or motivation—or
each can also be used as a springboard
for group discussion.

Surround yourself with friends you can share your hopes, dreams, sorrows and happiness with.

The first step in battling mental illness is talking about it—it's not always easy, but it is worth it.

———————————————————

NATALIE HARRIS

Take solace in just "being."

Your job is not to be a people-pleaser or a perfectionist. Remember, your happiness shouldn't depend on whether you make the people around you happy.

NATALIE HARRIS

Thoughts can dictate
how you feel. Unfortunately,
thoughts are not
always right.

When you move out of your comfort zone, you will see it wasn't actually comfortable at all.

NATALIE HARRIS

Bravery happens the moment the fighter enters the ring.

You are stronger than you
give yourself credit for.

NATALIE HARRIS

Be willing to accept the
help you need.

The journey can be full of huge highs and deep lows.

Set appropriate goals. You are allowed to have high expectations of yourself, but they need to be reasonable.

When someone compliments you, the only reply necessary is "Thank you."

NATALIE HARRIS

You don't need to pull A+'s
in life; you just need to show
up and keep trying—even
if you are late.

You are in charge of how
much power you give away.

NATALIE HARRIS

There isn't a magic pill
to fix feelings.

The grey areas in life can be frustrating. Work at trying to accept the grey.

NATALIE HARRIS

You determine your
own self-esteem.

Heartbreak is an emotion
we all feel.

NATALIE HARRIS

If you want to change your
life, you must change your
vision of your life.

You deserve to be loved and respected.

There are no such things as winners and losers; there are only winners and *learners.*

You are who you see in the mirror.

Feelings are not right
or wrong—feelings
simply exist.

Sometimes anxiety and panic may be signals that suppressed feelings are trying to emerge.

NATALIE HARRIS

Every feeling carries a charge of energy. When we hold that energy in and do not give it expression, it may create a state of tension.

If you continually suppress
your feelings, it can lead to
increased difficulty in
expressing or even
identifying them.

NATALIE HARRIS

Masking your true feelings
for most of your life never
works—truth is the only
path to healing.

Why ask "why?" when the best answer we can possibly come up with is an assumption at best?

NATALIE HARRIS

It is all perspective, my dear.

Be as vulnerable as you
need to be.

Be mindful and in
the moment.

Every small step leads to a healthier mind.

NATALIE HARRIS

Sometimes feelings are more intense when you begin to face situations you've been avoiding for a long time.

Try positive self-talk.

Take time to just be,
to just sit, to just accept,
to just breathe.

It's OK to set healthy boundaries.

We shouldn't need bravery
in order to talk about mental
illnesses—this belief is
killing us. Let's save bravery
for the challenges in our
lives and for the actual fight.

Give yourself permission to practise trusting yourself. Seek to understand your issues rather than let others shape how you think, feel and act.

NATALIE HARRIS

Speak for yourself and stand
behind your word.

If you have vices with serious consequences, you need to own them—or your consequences will be grave.

NATALIE HARRIS

Trust that distressful
feelings will pass.

Remind yourself every day that you can only fix yourself and no one else—stop managing others.

NATALIE HARRIS

Hiding your true self
is exhausting—and
unnecessary.

Be present and in the moment. Don't worry about the future or the past.

NATALIE HARRIS

Take responsibility for your own mistakes, unhappiness, future and personal growth.

You can make a plan, just don't plan the outcome.

NATALIE HARRIS

Putting a perfection stamp
on your near future is the
opposite of health. It's
possibly a recipe for disaster.

Your feelings don't, in
any way, discount your
gratefulness.

NATALIE HARRIS

Look for evidence before worrying.

Allow yourself the
opportunity to truly heal.

NATALIE HARRIS

Identify destructive behaviours, find alternative behaviours and implement them—and practise, practise, practise.

Self-pity is a huge demon.

NATALIE HARRIS

Your only responsibility
is to try.

Accept support.

Take time to clear
your mind.

Spirituality is an integral
part of recovery.

NATALIE HARRIS

Do what is healthy for
you right now.

Your broken shield can only last for so long, but if people don't know you're broken, they can't help you win your battle.

NATALIE HARRIS

Changing your outlook about people-pleasing even slightly doesn't mean you are rude and selfish; it means you are not forgetting to take care of yourself.

Sometimes acceptance is
a difficult but a necessary
pill to swallow.

NATALIE HARRIS

Routine helps the brain.

Although sometimes
you might feel this way,
remember you are not alone.

You are capable of eventually
gaining true freedom.

Vulnerability equals freedom.

NATALIE HARRIS

You don't have to fight the
demons in your head alone.

Security and money don't stop you from having challenges.

NATALIE HARRIS

Accept others for
who they are and for
their own choices.

When you allow yourself to crumble to pieces, the whole world doesn't fall apart with you.

NATALIE HARRIS

When possible, remove
yourself from negative people
who are personal triggers.

Tears can help heal you.

Making your outside world
perfect won't make your
inside world perfect too.

Recovery is a moment-by-moment mission.

NATALIE HARRIS

Everyone faces sadness that
they thought was never
even possible.

Avoiding pain is an
unhealthy way to behave
and often slowly leads
people into a horrible
depression.

NATALIE HARRIS

It is amazing what you can
learn about yourself when you
stop hiding from yourself.

End relationships with
people who make you feel
shame, guilt or less
than others.

Take a stand and rationally
challenge extreme judgments
right when they occur.

Putting negative labels on yourself can have long-lasting effects on your self-esteem.

Don't confuse your career
with your life. Explore who
you truly are minus
your profession.

Hard times don't
discriminate.

Resentment casts
you onto an island of
loneliness and anger with
the only ship to rescue
you called forgiveness.

Extreme thoughts can
sabotage relationships.

NATALIE HARRIS

Think about the
consequences any heat-
of-the-moment decisions
would have on your
entire life.

What is important in life
is never found in a box
with a bow.

NATALIE HARRIS

The way you cope with the atrocities of life is a choice.

Have a crisis plan and a
network of good friends.

NATALIE HARRIS

Mindfulness is awareness
in the moment, in the
here and now. It involves
being aware of what you
are doing and what you are
thinking about doing.

Making incorrect judgments
is part of being human.

Try not to fall back
into selfish behaviours
and previous negative
coping methods.

Love one another—that medicine never hurts.

NATALIE HARRIS

You will have to feel a
punch or two in life, rather
than numb yourself, in
order to grow.

Take things one day at a time
rather than ruminate about
the unknown future.

NATALIE HARRIS

Don't allow pride and fear
of ridicule to keep you
suffering in silence.

Don't shy away from a road
that may lead to fulfilled
dreams because the road is
unfamiliar to you.

NATALIE HARRIS

An all-or-nothing outlook
on life and love isn't rational.

You don't need to justify
your choices to anyone,
and you definitely don't need
to feel selfish for developing
healthy boundaries.

NATALIE HARRIS

One day at a time. One hour at a time. One minute at a time. One second at a time.

A little mixture of
mindfulness and
mindlessness is sometimes
the perfect balance.

NATALIE HARRIS

Love simply wishes
someone happiness and
wellness—that's it, that's
all—no hidden clauses or
fine print, no expiry dates
or restrictions applied.

Try to take back and use the power of your imagination.

When you share your
journey, you inspire others
to continue with theirs.

By putting a new view or "frame" on your experiences, you change the way you see them.

NATALIE HARRIS

Do give yourself
permission to forgive.

Lilac trees smell just
as wonderful when they
are wilting.

NATALIE HARRIS

When you are confused, it means you aren't complacent and are striving for lifelong improvement. Confusion equals effort.

Keep your eyes on the road.

NATALIE HARRIS

Live a life that maintains the
passionate wish to prolong
your health and well-being
without harsh expectations.

If you want to stay on the recovery path, you need to trust in your ability to get through hard times.

NATALIE HARRIS

Don't swim in shit soup.

Stop believing that only your opinion is correct.

Cultivating happiness
doesn't happen overnight.

Learn the importance of professional delegation and embrace the opportunity to gather feedback.

Take a moment to admire
the second chances all
around you.

Be addicted to love and
happiness.

Change can be terrifying
and very uncomfortable.
Fear of the unknown can
keep us from achieving
many successes—and also
can keep us from those
equally as important failures
we so desperately need to
learn from.

Remember the importance of humility.

NATALIE HARRIS

Let life guide you, rather
than trying to guide
life. When you always
have to be at the wheel,
you continue to crash into
resentment when things
don't go your way.

When you use your
imagination, you allow
yourself to go somewhere
else at this very moment.

NATALIE HARRIS

Learn to balance
perfectionism with
discovery.

Take small leaps of faith
and see things beyond your
own perspective.

NATALIE HARRIS

If you don't have
supportive family and
friends, get new ones.

Strangers can turn into
friends in all of a heartbeat.

NATALIE HARRIS

The main purpose of sharing life stories is to show that through the darkness there is light.

If you slow down and
read the directions, you
may see that your gut tells
you to turn an entirely
different way.

NATALIE HARRIS

Don't blame others for
your feelings.

There is no such thing as coincidences—life is like a platter of perfection masquerading as irony. At first it appears to serve a dish of disappointment, but if you look closely enough, it's actually serving exactly what you need.

NATALIE HARRIS

Instead of thinking that certain people and circumstances cause suffering, choose to perceive these people and events as opportunities to gain deeper insights into your own mind's misconceptions.

Don't let guilt trick you
into thinking tough love
will backfire on you.

NATALIE HARRIS

Attachment to an outcome
can only lead to jealousy,
envy and anger.

The first step to healing
is to have the willingness
and courage to open up to
someone you trust.

NATALIE HARRIS

When we are stagnant
because of our fear of change,
we block ourselves from life
and truly living.

Today you are already
enough.

~*Mandy Johnson*

There is always hope.

True gifts are found in
your heart, in hugs and in
cherished moments, because
you are blessed enough to
have them.

NATALIE HARRIS

You don't need to have the
answers right away.

All the compassion you
can provide will never alter
the universe's ultimate
outcome in a particular
situation. When things don't
go according to your wish,
remember it is out of
your hands.

NATALIE HARRIS

Let our boys cry too.

A perfectionist attitude does
not always serve you well.

NATALIE HARRIS

Validate the fears and
concerns of others.

In order to find the transformative jewel of love, you must deliberately take a stand to reverse negative tendencies of attachment and exchange them for new, positive, selfless habits.

NATALIE HARRIS

The world remains a much
better place when you don't
have to hide.

Give yourself time and permission to process a painful event.

NATALIE HARRIS

The bond of humanity
occurs when a heart
feels the pain of another
person's loss.

Talking about challenges
equates to strength and
leadership.

No one can "complete"
you or be the key to
your happiness.

Step up to the plate, stand
tall and do exactly what is
good for you.

The root of giving should
come from love—not
from the need for
acknowledgement.

Forgiveness is a two-way street. Whether someone forgives you is completely out of your control. But you can't forgive others and not forgive yourself.

NATALIE HARRIS

Grounding allows us to live
our life rather than run
from our life.

We often interchange
the word "love" with the
word "attachment"
without thinking.

NATALIE HARRIS

In the textbook of life,
there are no answers to
some important questions
no matter how hard
you study.

Confusion must be present
before wisdom can be born.

We all need patience, love
and hope along the way.

Hiding from situations in
life that cause conflict will
only cause more pain.

Through effort and
determination to stay on
the pathway to recovery, we
can gain life stability and
improve life outcomes.

Shit happens. At times
life sucks.

NATALIE HARRIS

When we label people in
extreme ways, they become
defensive because our
statements are unrealistic
and one-sided.

By having extreme false judgments about others and yourself, you create a self-fulfilling prophecy that destroys the relationships you want to keep.

NATALIE HARRIS

Remind yourself to be
patient with you.

Love is selfless, giving and
comes from a special home
in our heart.

NATALIE HARRIS

Make vulnerability your
new friend and see where
the possibilities of this
journey take you.

Take time to develop and
implement a game plan.

NATALIE HARRIS

Accept compliments every
time they are given.

Your imagination is the
passageway to all possibility.

NATALIE HARRIS

We need to allow ourselves
to experience all of the
normal human emotions
that may come with a
situation.

Even if your life is good,
it still takes hard work to
maintain.

NATALIE HARRIS

The sooner you accept
that it will take time to get
through a loss, the sooner
you will heal from it.

When we lash out with
extreme judgments, our
loved ones don't want to
make us feel loved
and secure.

NATALIE HARRIS

Recovery is a work
in progress.

Carry the lessons of your
past experiences in a pocket
closest to your heart,
but don't let them drag
you down and slow your
progress forward.

NATALIE HARRIS

It's OK to say "no."

It takes a lot of dedication
to change our old habits,
but the result is well
worth the effort.

NATALIE HARRIS

Life consists of seasons.

Relax a little and discover
new things that you may not
be the best in.

NATALIE HARRIS

Sadness is a normal
emotion.

You cannot simultaneously set a boundary and take care of another person's feelings.

NATALIE HARRIS

Extending forgiveness helps
you forgive yourself.

When your children are crying, they are sad. When they yell, they are mad—and those feelings are OK!

NATALIE HARRIS

You deserve every ounce
of love and self-care you
can receive.

Use mindfulness and
patience to navigate through
emotions rather than
pushing them away.

When we accuse people
of things they don't do,
it slams the door shut on
negotiation, causing hurt
and misunderstanding for
both parties involved.

Pure happiness comes from accepting ourselves with all our faults and blunders— and in the ability to give love to another human without hidden resentment, ill feelings or expectations.

NATALIE HARRIS

Some days your sparkle may
not be as bright as other
days, but it's always there.

We can't throw out our
family trees or turn back
the hands of time to avoid a
trauma, but we can choose
to see our pasts through
a different, more peaceful
perspective.

NATALIE HARRIS

You are your choices, not anyone else's.

Busy minds are crammed full of stuff, and calming the storm long enough to imagine something positive may take a bit of getting used to. But make it part of your nightly routine and it will become just that—*routine*!

NATALIE HARRIS

When you decide to set
a limit with someone,
you need to do it clearly,
without anger and using as
few words as possible.

Increase your spiritual connection.

Guilt can be a tangled
chain holding you back
from complete peace.

It is a gift to learn how to be present in the now and to experience every aspect of life.

NATALIE HARRIS

If we truly possess the
wish for everyone to be
happy and well, we would
never attach ourselves to
them—it simply wouldn't
be necessary.

The strongest bonds
are formed through the
realization that two people
have experienced the
same emotions—universal
emotions.

NATALIE HARRIS

Remember you're beautiful.
You're one of a kind.
~ *Adam Hunwicks*

Natalie Harris is the author of *Save-My-Life School.* She is a speaker, an educator, an advanced-care paramedic, a mental health advocate and the creator of a peer-support group called Wings of Change. Please visit her blog, *Paramedic Nat's Mental Health Journey,* or listen to her podcast, BrainStorm.

CONNECT

 paramedicnatsmentalhealthjourney.com

 savemylifeschool

 paramedicnat1

 paramedicnat1

 savemylifeschoolbook.com